THE DOG'S BARK
Simple Truths from a Wise Pet

Bill Zimmerman
 Illustrated by Tom Bloom

WILLOW CREEK PRESS
Minocqua, Wisconsin

© 2003 Bill Zimmerman
Illustrations © Tom Bloom

Editor: Andrea Donner
Design: Katrin Wooley

Published by Willow Creek Press
P.O. Box 147, Minocqua, Wisconsin 54548
www.willowcreekpress.com

Originally published as *Dog-Mas: Simple Truths from a Wise Pet* in 1995 by Hazelden.

Library of Congress Cataloging-in-Publication Data:
Zimmerman, William 1941-
    The dog's bark : simple truths from a wise pet / Bill Zimmerman ;
illustrations by Tom Bloom.
        p. cm.
    ISBN 1-57223-685-X (hardcover : alk. paper)
1. Dogs-- Humor. 2. Conduct of life--Humor. 3. Dogs--Pictorial works.
4. Dogs--Caricatures and cartoons. I. Title.
    PN6231.D68Z56 2003
    818' .5402--dc21   2003002526

Printed in Canada

For my daughter,
Carlota,
who with open heart
found Dynamite
and saved her
life.
And for Dynamite,
who has given
us all only love in
return.

—BILL ZIMMERMAN

PAW-WORD

My dog, Dynamite, comforts me in the early morning just with her presence. She comes to me to love her, to touch and pet her. I give this willingly, for in comforting her, giving her ballast, I find my own grounding for the day.

My dog has always shown me all the kindness of her nature, never holding back, constant and generous in seeing me through personal losses. Hard as I might try, I could never be as unselfish and kind as she. How privileged I am to know Dynamite.

My little dog has taught me how to have fun, to relax more, and to enjoy the fine weather and new grass. She has shown me what loyalty is. In short, she has helped me become a better human being.

I wrote this book to share with you the wisdom I have learned from Dynamite. I try to imagine what words she would use, if she could, to impart her simple truths. Follow them and they will show you, as they have me, how to live a better life.

Bill Zimmerman

DOGSCENTS

WAYS TO APPROACH LIFE

GO OUT INTO THE WORLD
INQUISITIVELY,
SNIFF, SNIFF
ALL AROUND YOU WITH
PASSION.
THERE ARE SO MANY GOOD
SMELLS.

A
>>DYNAMITE<<
THOUGHT

GREET EACH DAY WITH HOPE AND EXPECTATION, WIPE FROM YOUR MEMORY ANY HURT OR SLIGHT FROM THE DAY BEFORE. BY DOING SO, YOU SET A GOOD EXAMPLE FOR YOUR HUMANS.

© Isabelle Francais

EVERY PUDDLE
IS AN OPPORTUNITY.

DON'T MISS ANY.

7

ALWAYS FIND
TIME TO PLAY.

© RonKimballStock.com

8

REMEMBER TO
SHARE THE QUIET
WITH SOMEONE
YOU LOVE.

© Henry H. Holdsworth

9

© RonKimballStock.com

GET LOTS
OF EXERCISE
AND SLEEP, AND
DRINK PLENTY
OF WATER.

11

SOMETIMES YOU JUST HAVE TO GIVE UP ON CHEWING THE SAME OLD BONE. KNOW WHEN TO START ON A NEW ONE.

© Norvia Behling

SHAKE OFF THE DAY.
NOW STRETCH AND RELAX.

(EVEN ROLL ON THE RUG.)

© Norvia Behling

13

BONE MOTS

IF YOU WANT TO BE NOTICED, LEAVE CLUES ALL AROUND.

(GOOD WORDS)

© Norvia Behling

RUN AFTER A SQUIRREL OR TWO. YOU DON'T HAVE TO CATCH ANY, BUT IT WILL BE FUN FOR A WHILE. (PANT, PANT)

© RonKimballStock.com

15

A »DYNAMITE« THOUGHT

WHEN YOU GET SOAKED, SHAKE YOURSELF DRY. PREPARE FOR ANOTHER GO ROUND.

© SpartasPhoto.com

STUDY THE HUMANS YOU MEET BEFORE COMMITTING TO THEM.

SNIFF THEM.
TILT YOUR HEAD.
BE PATIENT.
THEY WILL
COME AROUND
IN TIME.

17

WE EACH NEED TO BE AROUND OTHERS. NEVER STAY ALONE FOR TOO LONG.

© SpartasPhoto.com

19

KEEP SOME FAVORITE TOYS NEARBY. YOU NEVER KNOW WHEN YOU'LL NEED THEM IN A MOMENT OF UNCERTAINTY OR SADNESS.

© Karen Hudson

A »Dynamite« Thought

© Norvia Behling

23

ALWAYS BE CURIOUS.

THERE'S SO MUCH
TO SEE AND LEARN.

© Nancy McCallum

24

TEST THE WATERS WITH A PAW ...

...BEFORE
PLUNGING IN.

© DenverBryan.com

25

BONE MOTS

LEAVE YOUR MARK
ON THIS WORLD.
WHEREVER. WHENEVER.
HOWEVER.

CITY DOG

COUNTRY DAWG

© Close Encounters of the Furry Kind

KNOW WHEN TO RETREAT.

TO DO SO WITH PRIDE IS STILL A VICTORY.

© Bill Buckley

A ›Dynamite‹ Thought

BE PREPARED TO GROWL OR BARE YOUR TEETH TO PROTECT WHAT IS YOURS. SAVE BITING AS A LAST RESORT.

© Jean M. Fogle

REMEMBER TO ROLL
OVER AND LOOK
AT LIFE FROM A NEW
PERSPECTIVE.

© Bonnie Nance

29

TAKE LONG WALKS.

THEY ARE GOOD
FOR YOU AND
CLEAR THE SOUL.

© Mark Anderman / Terry W ld Studio

31

MAINTAIN A CORE OF INDEPENDENCE. THIS WILL MAKE HUMANS RESPECT YOU MORE . . .

© Terry Wild Studio

. . . AND APPRECIATE YOUR STRONG NATURE.

TAKE COMFORT IN YOUR HEARTH. IT CAN BE COLD OUTSIDE, YOU KNOW.

© Kent & Donna Dannen

35

TRY TO BE OBEDIENT . . .

© RonKimballStock.com

BUT DON'T FORGET TO
RUN THROUGH A FLOCK
OF PIGEONS NOW AND
THEN. THEY'RE TOO
PRECIOUS TO RESIST
AND YOU NEED YOUR
DAILY QUOTA OF FUN.

BONE MOTS

EAT WHEN FOOD IS OFFERED.
YOUR NEXT MEAL
MAY NOT COME SO EASILY.

© Norvia Behling

WHEN A LOVED ONE COMES HOME, DO A LITTLE DANCE OF JOY FOR THEM. MAKE THEM SMILE.

ARF, ARF.

39

ALWAYS KISS
THE HAND THAT
FEEDS YOU.
OR AT LEAST
GIVE IT A LICK.

© SpartasPhoto.com

BE LOYAL TO THOSE WHO FIRST DISCOVERED AND NURTURED YOU. NEVER BETRAY THEM. IT'S NOT GOOD TO BE FICKLE.

© SpartasPhoto.com

BE LOVING TO AND PROTECTIVE OF THOSE WHO ARE KIND TO YOU.

© Terry Wild Studio

43

ALWAYS STAND BY THE ONE YOU LOVE, AND REMEMBER TO LICK THEIR FACE.

© Kent & Donna Dannen

(SLURP)

BE GENTLE AND KIND.
THERE IS ALREADY SO
MUCH PAIN IN OUR WORLD.

© Alan & Sandy Carey

45

RUB UP AGAINST SOMEONE WHO LOVES YOU. NUZZLE THEM. (NMMNMM)

© Terry Wild Studio

46

BE UNSELFISH IN YOUR LOVE.

© Norvia Behling

REMEMBER,
YOU ARE NOT THE CAT.

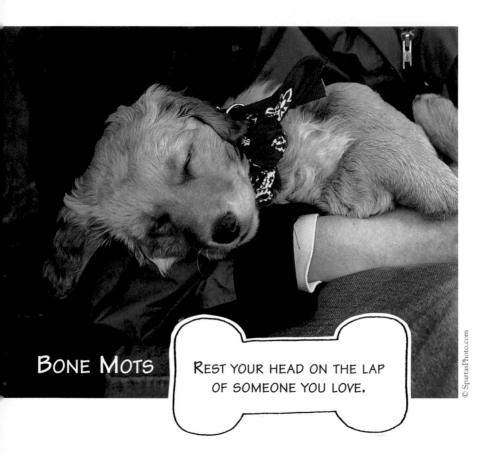

BONE MOTS

REST YOUR HEAD ON THE LAP
OF SOMEONE YOU LOVE.

© SpartasPhoto.com

Don't be sad when the humans you love leave you behind. They will return because of their love. Have faith in them.

© SpartasPhoto.com

49

TEND TO THE NEEDS OF YOUR HUMAN WHO COMES IN WET FROM THE RAIN.

51

A BIT OF KIBBLE FROM AN ARFLETIC TRAINER:

SEE SPOT RUN IN PLACE, STRETCH, SPOT, STRETCH.

BEING RESPONSIBLE TO OTHERS IS A RESPONSIBILITY OF YOURS. GO FOR IT!

© DenverBryan.com

A BIT OF KIBBLE FROM A PAWLICE OFFICER:

Fight for what is right.
Don't shirk
from your duty
to yourself and your humans.

IF YOU BRING
PUPPIES INTO
THE WORLD,
BE PREPARED
TO TAKE CARE
OF THEM WHILE
THEY GROW UP.

© Norvia Behling

YOU CAN WANDER AND MEANDER, BUT BEWARE! EVENTUALLY YOU HAVE TO COME HOME.

GIVE COMFORT TO THE HUMANS YOU LOVE.

© Bill Buckley

THEY NEED SO MUCH CARE.
REMEMBER THAT THEY ALWAYS
COMFORT YOU WHEN YOU WHIMPER
IN YOUR SLEEP. NMNMM.

61

BE AFFECTIONATE.
NEVER BE RESTRAINED
IN YOUR LOVE. (SLURP)

YOU WILL FIND SOME GOOD IN ALL HUMANS
IF YOU WAIT LONG ENOUGH.

A BIT OF KIBBLE FROM A PAWTRAIT PAINTER:

© Terry Wild Studio

BE WISE. EVEN IF SOMEONE YOU LOVE HURTS YOU, STICK BY THEM. THEY'LL COME TO THEIR SENSES. YOU BE THE SMART ONE.

67

BE PRACTICAL. KNOW WHEN TO BARK, WHEN TO YELP, WHEN TO WHINE, AND ABOVE ALL, KNOW WHEN TO BE QUIET.

© DusanSmetana.com

SOME PRACTICAL POINTERS

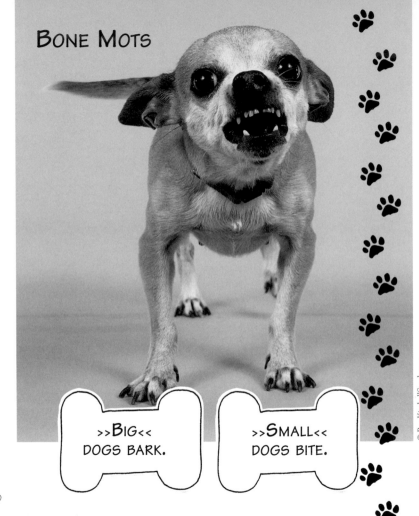

BONE MOTS

>>BIG<< DOGS BARK.

>>SMALL<< DOGS BITE.

© RonKimballStock.com

CULTIVATE YOUR ABILITY
TO FALL ASLEEP
AT THE DROP OF A HAT.
AND NAP, NAP, NAP.

© Lynn M. Stone

ONE CAN RARELY GET TOO MANY NAPS. (YAWN)

TAKE TIME
TO GROOM
YOURSELF.
KEEP CLEAN.

© Tara Darling

A >>DYNAMITE<< THOUGHT

SHOW THE WORLD WHEN YOU ARE HAPPY. (WAG YOUR TAIL IF YOU HAVE ONE.) HUMANS LIKE SIGNS TELLING THEM HOW YOU FEEL.

© RonKimballStock.com

BE SMART.
LEARN TO SPEAK UP,
WHEN TO BEG, AND
EVEN HOW TO
ROLL OVER AND
PLAY DEAD.

© Tara Darling

FIND A FAVORITE SPOT
SOMEWHERE,
AND MAKE IT YOURS.

79

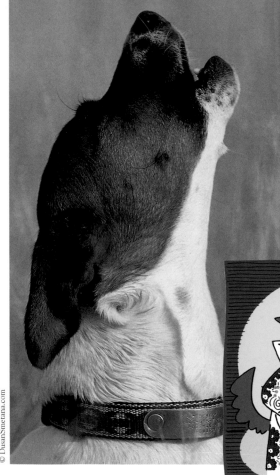

SOMETIMES,
YOU JUST
HAVE TO YIP,
BARK
AND HOWL
TO RID YOUR
SOUL OF ITS
DEMONS.
BE WILD ONCE
IN A WHILE.

A BIT OF KIBBLE FROM A BARKEOLOGIST:

CONSTRUCT YOUR LIFE
PIECE BY PIECE,
ONE DAY AT A TIME.

© Bill Buckley

BONE MOTS

TALE OF A TAIL:
WAG IT IF YOU'RE GLAD,
DRAG IT IF YOU'RE SAD.

© DenverBryan.com

© Kent & Donna Dannen

FEAR NOT THE BIG SNEEZE; IT'S A HEALTHY WAY TO CLEAR YOUR HEAD. TROUBLES CAN BE SHAKEN AWAY, TOO.

KNOW WHEN
TO BARE YOUR FANGS
AND CLAWS.

DON'T LET OTHERS
ABUSE YOU.

© DusanSmetana.com

PLAN YOUR FUTURE.

KNOW WHERE
YOU'RE GOING.

BUT BE AWARE OF
WHAT'S FOLLOWING YOU.

© SpartasPhoto.com

89

BONE MOTS

BE GENTLE WITH ALL HUMANITY.

© Close Encounters of the Furry Kind

Don't worry if you have dog breath. It doesn't mean you're not lovable. You are; you know it.

EVERY DOG HAS ITS DAY.
SO REST UP, YOURS
JUST MAY BE ON THE WAY.

© Alan & Sandy Carey

93

BILL ZIMMERMAN, *the creator of* The Dog's Bark, *has been a questioner all his life. A journalist for more than twenty years and a prize-winning editor, Zimmerman is special projects editor for* Newsday, *one of the nation's largest newspapers. His other books are* The Little Book of Joy: An Interactive Journal for Thoughts, Prayers, and Wishes; How to Tape Instant Oral Biographies, *a book that teaches you how to capture your family stories on audio and video tape;* Make Beliefs, *a magical gift book for the imagination;* Lifelines: A Book of Hope, *which offers comforting thoughts;* A Book of Questions to Keep Thoughts and Feelings, *a new form of diary/journal; and* The Cat's Meow: Feline Answers to Life's BIG Questions, *also published by Willow Creek Press.*

Tom Bloom has worked doggedly for a number of years doing drawings in a fetching style. He's paper trained, with work appearing in The New York Times, Newsday, The New Yorker, Barron's, Fortune, Games and others. He has received all shots, is good with kids, and has never bitten anyone. Currently, he and his mate board in New York with the pups.

SHARE WITH US

Dear Reader,

Please share with us the simple truths you have learned from your own pet. Perhaps we can incorporate some of them in future editions. We also welcome your comments and suggestions to make The Dog's Bark funnier and wiser. Please

Bill Zimmerman
Guarionex Press
201 West 77 Street
New York, NY 10024.
email:wmz@aol.com